SWITCH SYSTEMS

BY
STEVEN J. NEWTON, SR.

Editor in Chief: Christian S. Newton
B.S in Criminal Justice
M.S in Adult, Occupation & Continuing Education

Project Manager: Dione C. Simmons
B.S. Biological Science
M.S. Psychology, Leadership Coaching

Book Cover Design: TKCG Information & Graphic Design Department

Please note the Embassy Publishing Centre capitalizing certain pronouns in scripture, that refer to the Father, Son and Holy Spirit and may differ from some publishers.

Take note that the name satan and related names are not capitalized. We choose not to acknowledge him even to the point of violating grammatical rules.

www.SJNSR.com

ISBN-13: 978-0-692-04892-4

Embassy Publishing

CONTENTS

INTRODUCTION

<u>I'm Delighted to Make Your Acquaintance</u>

As I received the revolutionary impulse to pen this, I wondered where to do I begin. So, I had to sit for a while and connect to the frequency of Kingdom Intelligence in which the great Apostle Paul identifies as the "*mind of Christ.*" Those three small words are EXTREMELY huge. Literally and esoterically, they carry explosive weights of glory in each vibrational frequency.

Now, you must travel with me to another level of consciousness to grasp an in-depth, non-religious understanding of what I will present to you. If you only perceive with a thought process simply birthed from Sunday School or Vacation Bible School, you will not understand the gravitational pull that is about to call you onto another floor: a higher floor of the elevator of your thinking. While those institutions of training were wonderful, fun, and share great memories, we must remember, they are also foundational. As believers, we were never meant to remain at cheese crackers, cookies, and Hawaiian Punch. We can't remain there! Regardless of the perceived difficult personal responsibilities placed upon us to move beyond it. It is imperative that we move from information to revelation. This particular level of awareness is going to pull you from the external systems of this world, into the internal systems that are unknowingly operating within you.

Many of you reading this, are aware of the powers operating within you, but you've heard so much, it's become difficult to harness those powers. It gets irritating to know that there is a force within, that you can use to manifest the lifestyle of God's best in this earth and can't quite figure out how to actuate it. Because of the rapid development, advancement, maturation, and stimulating unfolding of consciousness globally, information overload can be a hindrance as well. This apostolic treatise, is written simply to serve as a budding flower in your hand. As you permit it to bloom, blossom, and bear fruit within you, you will transition into another reality that is and has always been at work within you. You just didn't have a conscious awareness of how to properly appropriate it, to manifest the desires of your heart.

Time has brought us together at this moment. A threshold of complications, frustrations, mistakes, embarrassments, problems, snares, and many other complexities have been reached, and a convergence is taking place. This is the reason most people get acquainted with an apostolic force. You are at a turning point: a point some would consider a crisis. Whether it be physically, emotionally, socially, relationally, financially, or spiritually; there is a calling for you to level up, grow up, and GO UP!

When Jesus was speaking to his disciples in Luke 22, He shared with them something extremely preeminent.

> "*And he said unto them, Behold, when ye are entered into the city, there shall a man meet you, bearing a pitcher of water; follow him into the house where he entereth in.* [11] *And ye shall say unto the goodman of the house, The Master saith unto thee, Where is the guestchamber, where I shall eat the passover with my disciples?* [12] *And he shall shew you a large upper room furnished: there make ready.*" Luke 22:10-12 KJV

Jesus was speaking of a transcendence that was going to take place. In other words: when you get into the city, the new place Jesus is sending you, you will find a man with a water pitcher. In another passage of scripture in Matthew 5, Jesus informs us that you and I are *"cities sat on a hill that can't be hid"* so we are the city that we're to go into. OMG, it's about to get crazy!! He says, *"follow that man"* and go upstairs with him to the upper room. Water is something we can drink and serve as a mode of travel. The pitcher is the container that holds the drink and method of travel. The upper-room is an indication of going higher. Jesus is expressing to His disciples then, and us now, that we are about to transcend and rise above the external systems of this world that have held us hostage as individuals, communities of people, and nations. We're about to ascend above the lower level frequencies of this world that has been the cause of tremendous suffering around the world.

This water is going to transport each and every one of us into a flow of creativity, harmony, purpose, light, and generosity like we've never seen it before. The level of power that is about to offered to you in this writing, will authentically catapult you into exceptional heights, where the painful memories of those who have abused this power through relational, religious, political, economical and other forms of institutional oppression will be abolished. You are about to shifted, shipped, and sent from victim to victor to vehicle.

You must choose to follow the man with the water pitcher into the house. However, with your decision to do that, comes the faith to experience and express the ultimate power of the government of God at work within you. Ultimately making you consciously attuned to the divine will of God for your life.

Welcome into the house! Come on upstairs and have a drink of refreshing, revitalizing, and restorative water in which you will absolutely, unequivocally, never thirst again.

Chapter One

Our Future Will Always Be God's Past

For I know the thoughts that I think toward you, saith the Lord, thoughts of peace, and not of evil, to give you an expected end. Jeremiah 29:11 KJV

What if I told you that your end was already expected? There is a clear pathway for your life. You just have to come into alignment with it. Your future has already been played out in the mind of God, the great architect of the universe. When you begin to flow with the journey as an individual, collectively massive transformation will take place. Your belief system however, will torment the experiences on your path if left unaddressed by remaining at a foundational level of spiritual thinking. You have to understand that the relationship you shared with God at six should not be the same relationship at twenty-six and sixty-six. The relationship develops as your knowledge of God develops. That shouldn't always have to be through struggle, hardships, temptations, tests, and trials. Without these complexities, there should be a pull to explore deeper levels with God. Might I suggest, many of our temptations, tests, trials, struggles, and pains are consequences to us ignoring that very pull?

The time or level of consciousness we are currently enclosed in is crucial. Globally loyalties are being demanded from all frontiers. Physically, emotionally, financially, politically, academically, and relationally. We are presently confronted by a deep refusal to move beyond what has been, into what God has already completed and what we will come to know as our future. Embracing this future is going to take a level of pro-activity and productivity that many of us have never known. To experience this future from a prosperous position, one must heed their ear to those who have given rise to the mind of God regarding the current. You can no longer cosign your past. Your life's story must be encapsulated in God's past which will always turn out to be your future.

You must begin to allocate your time so that you can be sufficient to accomplish what God has assigned you to do-- the very purpose for which you were sent to this earth. Your rewards, payoffs, and provisions are dormant within an unfinished project that God started within you. The payment of your bills is resting in an idea that you have procrastinated with. Your provision has been tucked away because you have been focused on your past or the past of others and not focused on God's past: which is your future.

There is a revolutionary, planetary move taking place. Remarkable advances in the heavenlies are being released that must be heard, embraced, and activated within your life at an accelerated pace. Many of you are behind time and if you don't get to work, you're going to miss the impact and influence that you have been assigned to make in the world. If you are spiritually connected in any way, you can sense God's global footprint clamping down on history right now. You can feel the gravitational pull to greater, better, empowerment and enrichment.

I know you can feel Bigger, Better, and Greater pulling at you right NOW!

Your belief system will torment the experiences on your path however. Take the idea that your path is just a roadway into the Garden of Eden. Eden is that place of freedom. That limitless space around you. Spread your arms right now! Feel the openness around you. That my friend is Eden! Wake up to how much room is left for you to, like Adam and Eve, run around naked and explore. Now you talk about self expression. You talk about authentic expression. Here is permission to be yourself. Here is your permission to be unique! Here is your permission to be free!

This is a freedom that never ends. This is a freedom that is multitudinous. This is boundless an infinite expression of who you were created to be. This is multifarious liberty. This is an open expression to liberate the element of God that you represent. See we are all small pieces of God in the earth, representing Him as little gods in the earth. Little atoms or beings of royalty that make up a whole.

You must begin however, to open your eyes to new worlds and spheres of influences that are opening up to us all. This is an invitation for healing. The problem is that Holy Spirit can't speak to an unwelcoming host. Light can't shine within someone who doesn't want it to. When you keep putting shades on or covering your windows where you or no one else can see inside, darkness wins. God knows nothing of darkness. God is light. You are light! Your frustration keeps appearing because you've learned to function in darkness and it's getting on your nerves. Darkness is ignorance, and it's time to turn the light on and leave it on.

> *You groped your way through that murk once, but no longer. You're out in the open now. The bright light of Christ makes your way plain. So no more stumbling around. Get on with it! The good, the right, the true—these*

are the actions appropriate for daylight hours. Figure out what will please Christ, and then do it. Don't waste your time on useless work, mere busywork, the barren pursuits of darkness. Expose these things for the sham they are. It's a scandal when people waste their lives on things they must do in the darkness where no one will see. Rip the cover off those frauds and see how attractive they look in the light of Christ. Wake up from your sleep, Climb out of your coffins; Christ will show you the light! So watch your step. Use your head. Make the most of every chance you get. These are desperate times! (Ephesians 5:8-16 MSG)

You cannot live an inspired, motivated, and high impact life in darkness. A life in darkness is delayed, depressing, agitating, and unproductive. You produce no fruit at all. All the fruit you seem to produce when in darkness, are those you happen to stumble into because of a fall. Because there was no light, you tripped over a shoe and saw a cookie while falling. Since you were down, you picked it up and marked it as a treat for falling. That little bit of goodness that you experienced while down was NOT God's best for your life. That wasn't a prize and lure to remain in consistent struggle.

When you fully grasp a hold of this and embrace this new reality of mental and spiritual expansion and integration, you create Eden or Heaven right here, right now. When you expand your ability to receive more from God, you not only live in harmony, but you began to release that harmony into the world. To be in this place is a choice. It's a decision! My friend, you can't break the rules of any reality you decide to be in. If you decide to be in the reality of suffering, to be free, you can't break the rules of that reality. If you desire to live in the reality of poverty, you can't break the rules of lack and live in its comforts of not being taxed. That reality is going to tax you. Whichever reality you choose, will tax you.

God created the universe, and you live in it. God created rules for this universe to operate, and as a result, the universe doesn't care if you struggle or not. The universe doesn't care if you suffer or not. All the universe knows is that the sun is rising on time, the moon and the stars will shine on cue. The rain will start and stop when directed. The birds will not bark, they will continue to chirp. The rooster will crow in the morning and the cow will continue to moo and never fly. Everything under the engagement of the universal power of God, will do as it's suppose to. When you choose to break the rules, you choose to suffer.

As a speaking spirit, we either have dominion, or we are under dominion. We cannot be neutral. We were created to be dominated by no force except the Divine Mind of Christ. We were created to be conquerors over any power or influence before us. The only force that is supposed to dominate you is the Divine Mind of Christ! You were created to dominate and conquer the powers and influences externally that would lead you astray from the kingdom that Jesus says is within you.

This power which is called dominion is available to every believer. The decision is yours! Decide to be victorious in Jesus! Some people, however, refuse to exercise the dominion God has given them through Christ Jesus. They are afraid to step out and take authority over the problem areas of their lives. I beg of you, do not be one of those people.

This was always God's will for you! It was in His thoughts when He made you. If you can believe this, and walk confidently knowing this, the thoughts God had about you in His past, can become your future and blow your mind.

Chapter Two

The Government of Everywhere

I was in the Junior Reserve Officers Training Corps (JROTC) all four years of my high school studies. I loved it so much, I joined the United States Army while I was still in high school. I elected to serve our country for over a decade. I've been privileged to travel all over the world. It was quite the experience. I started preaching at 7 years old in my mother's front yard and have been preaching ever since. I've been a "preacher-boy" all of my life. I was the young boy in middle school with a briefcase instead of a backpack. I was the little boy who would show up to Sunday School in the intermediate class with commentaries and systematic theology books. If there is anything I know, I know the Bible. If there was any career I enjoyed, I loved the Army.

Little did I know that the two would collide. I was able to live in Europe for six years and in Iraq for fifteen months. I called that my backside of the desert experience. When I wasn't dodging bullets and bombs, burning poop and trash, pulling shower duties, or keeping my area clean in my tent, I was deep into the word of God. It was here that God began to open my eyes to a lot. I had the experience to wash my clothes in the river of Euphrates. I saw, with my own eyes, signs that would say, Welcome to Babylon. Though it was a terrible position and just the absolute wrong time for me to be there, the scriptures became absolutely real to me.

I remember calling my great-grandmother who is ninety-six, at the time of this writing. She was encouraging me in the bunker saying, "the same God who protected you over here, is protecting you there baby. I'll see you when you get home." Unfortunately, others did not make it home, but thanks be to God, the rest of my unit and I did. However, when I came home, my spiritual perspective was completely different for many reasons. One because that statement was extremely true. The same God that was protecting me while growing up in the United States, in Europe, and then in war in Iraq was protecting me the whole time. If that be true, and I believed and still believe it is, why would I be comfortable in getting enjoyment out of killing my brothers and sisters? How could I continue to find peace in blowing up their streets and villages? What made the killing we did under the orders of our leaders acceptable to God, more so than the guy who killed his neighbor over an argument of ten dollars on the street corner? If I was preaching them to this hell, wasn't I on my way too? It got real to me!

I prided myself on never smoking a cigarette, drinking alcohol, clubbing, running women, and all of these other external sins we point out in ministry that we may or may not be doing while condemning others. What made what I was doing in uniform better than any of that? In that fashion, I wasn't helping the expansion of the God's global plan of restoring Eden in the earth. I was only a pawn in the plot of a democratic plan in which as a black citizen of the United States, I barely get to experience myself.

It was then, after preaching it for years, that the words of Jesus LEAPED into my spirit. *Neither shall they say, Lo here! or, lo there! for, behold, the kingdom of God is within you*. Luke 17:21 KJV I begin to study this kingdom that Jesus, the person I said I had been following for years talked about. Unfortunately, there are many others presently, who like me, knew Jesus, loved Jesus, followed Jesus, yet had no idea of this kingdom Jesus spoke of. Our only attachment to this kingdom was the church we attended. Boy, was I mistaken! I thank God for the institution of the church. The authentic body of Christ; not what the majority of us have come to know as the business of collecting people and leaving them mentally bound all under the guise of the glory of God. I'm talking about the church, the "called out ones" that Jesus actually was speaking of.

If you really study this word "church" out, and go beyond the Greek into the actual Latin language: you'll find the term orchestra. This was not the symphonic band that comes to mind. This orchestra was a place where the dignitaries were seated. It was where the senators and governing officials were seated in public places. So when Jesus was saying, "upon this rock, I'll build my church," He was speaking of another form of government. He was speaking of the orchestra. He was speaking of a people who operated under another rule of law. This government was prophesied about in the Old Testament, but because of our one-dimensional grasp of the text, we only used it for Christmas cards, speeches, and skits in the church.

For unto us a child is born, unto us a son is given: and the government shall be upon his shoulder: and his name shall be called Wonderful, Counsellor, The mighty God, The everlasting Father, The Prince of Peace. 7 *Of the increase of his government and peace there shall be no end, upon the throne of David, and upon his kingdom, to order it, and to establish it with judgment and with justice from henceforth even for ever. The zeal of the Lord of hosts will perform this.* Isaiah 9:6-7 KJV

This prophetic word speaks to the increase of this government; His government. What government was this speaking of? This was beyond democratic, republican, libertarian, and independents. This was beyond something that could be voted on. There was another system God was endeavoring to make us aware of. This same system my great-grandmother in her vast yet limited knowledge released when she said, "the same God who protected you over here, is protecting you there baby. I'll see you when you get home."

There was an Iraqi grandmother saying the same thing to her grandson. There is an Israeli grandmother saying the same thing to her grandson. There is a Pakistani grandmother saying the same thing to her grandson. If all our grandmothers are telling us the same thing, whose grandmother is lying? I'm tearing up as I write this. I remember as a boy preacher, I was fourteen at the time, and had given so much of my childhood to ministry and studying the scriptures from cover to cover, I asked my mother why do we have denominations. What is the purpose of religions? I mean I was raised under a pastor who spoke nine languages fluently. He had also given his life to the gospel ministry. So, I had to be on top of my game. When I started preaching, he didn't give me a check. He gave me books to go and study. My mother taught me to read at three. I knew I was comprehending, it's just that what I read and what I saw in the earth and just in my neighborhood didn't match. I can remember at the young age of fifteen preaching a sermon, "Can't We All Just Get Along?"

It dawned on me that God wasn't into religion. God could care less about any of our denominations. There was a larger system at operation here and Jesus talked about it most. I grew up defending Jesus, and faith in Him. Now I defend Jesus, faith in Him, and what He actually released to us and it was not a religion. It was a government and this government was everywhere. The liberty in knowing that there is not spot where God is not is exhilarating. This is what the angel was speaking of when it said, "And the angel said unto them, Fear not: for, behold, I bring you good tidings of great joy, which shall be to all people." Luke 2:10 KJV

This great joy is to ALL people. This is not a Baptist message. This is not a Pentecostal message. This is not a Hindu or Muslim message! This is not a denominational or religious message! The message of the kingdom and the royal family brings joy to ALL people. My goodness did we get off track. It's not supposed to just bring joy to the people who look like you and talk like you; who live where you live or drive what you drive. It brings joy to all people.

It is time for us all to switch systems! When your mind and your spirit come into alignment with this, your body will become the gateway to God's best. The Garden of Eden can flow through you. When you walk by the spirit, in this system, it liberates you from survival issues and you no longer allow financial, political, health, relationship concerns to occupy your mind on monopolize your attention.

Our worldview is made up of beliefs: opinions or convictions that we see as truth. The kinds of beliefs we carry with us influence the kinds of thoughts we have on both the conscious and unconscious level. They also affect our behavior, and our relationships with others and the world. When we entered this earth, we were meant to forever feed from the feast of the all-knowing, all powerful, and omnipresent source of creation we call God. Hunger, thirst, lack, poverty and any form of insufficiency were never a part of the plan. The explosion that takes place within when you realize the answers to our global pain is within us. God's government is everywhere!

Chapter Three

Kingdom: The Gold Mine

This information is what they never wanted you to know. It's the systemic solution to every problem we face globally. Our problem is that, we have held an idea of it in our minds while never attempting to actually function in it. It never became real to us to even try to appropriate it. It was just a bible story and history lessons.

> *"Since this is the kind of life we have chosen, the life of the Spirit, let us make sure that we do not just hold it as an idea in our heads or a sentiment in our hearts, but work out its implications in every detail of our lives. That means we will not compare ourselves with each other as if one of us were better and another worse. We have far more interesting things to do*

with our lives. Each of us is an original." Galatians 5:25-26 MSG

This is an extremely powerful position to be in. Power has been abused for so long, that it may cause you to have second thoughts about pursing this power that is at work within you. *"Now unto Him that is able to do exceeding abundantly above all that we ask or think,* ***according to the power that worketh in us****."* Ephesians 3:20 KJV If you don't have a clue about that power, then exceeding, abundantly cannot be attained. It will just be something we continue to shout about, dance for, speak in tongues, run around the building and yet never experience it in this physical life. We don't need the power working in us in Heaven. We won't need it then. We need that power in operation right here on this earth.

It is humankind's misuse of power that has caused great suffering. So, for many, this writing is a threat to their lifestyles. They have been living good lives off your ignorance and fear. However, in order to avoid self-destruction and the destruction of entire communities of people, we must CRY ALOUD! This type of power, only a concentrated few knew of before. Left to that, the rest of us, were left powerless. A complete victim of the society we lived in. Jesus changed that when He came with the system of the Kingdom of God!

This is why they killed Him. Right, I said it, THEY KILLED HIM! I know…we were taught to say, He gave up His life because no man takes His life. No, they didn't take the LIFE that came from God, of course not, that life is eternal! But oh yes, they took His physical life. That cross came from people who have given us many of the spiritual practices we have grown to love. That crown of thorns came from people who did not desire that He inform us that there was a greater power at work within us, that superseded any type of power they attempted to hold over our heads. It's okay though, in that Bible they gave us, which for many became a tool of oppression, there is a scripture in there, that will release you from that vice.

> *Thou hast caused men to ride over our heads; we went through fire and through water: but thou broughtest us*

out into a wealthy place. Psalms 66:12 KJV

You made men (charioteers) [a]ride over our heads [in defeat]; We went through fire and through water, Yet You brought us out into a [broad] place of abundance [to be refreshed]. Psalms 66:12 AMP

He trained us first, passed us like silver through refining fires,
Brought us into hardscrabble country, pushed us to our very limit,
Road-tested us inside and out, took us to hell and back;
Finally he brought us to this well-watered place. Psalms 66:12 MSG

In all three versions, it's laid out flat for you: plain and simple. You have to want to misunderstand it to misunderstand it. Those around you may have used their power in a negative way and abused it. You have power within you however, to rise above all that, and enter into a great place of refreshment, abundance, and surplus. Glory to God! When you decide to switch systems, you're making a choice to live in the Garden of Eden. Eden must become your chamber of residence again. The energy of Eden must become the vehicle for which you move and have your being.

A radical shift has taken place on the inside of you right now! Yep, that feeling you feel is a new vision of yourself no longer being under the forces of political and spiritual overlords. You are beginning to awaken to the precious power of the Kingdom of God that Jesus spoke of so much. My friend, your territory will never enlarge beyond your capacity to think. I'm not speaking of your possessions, but your territory. I'm speaking of something much larger than possessions! I'm speaking your dominion of space, thought, essence, & time. This is colossal!

> *"So from now on we regard no one from a worldly point of view. Though we once regarded Christ in this way, we do so no longer. Therefore, if anyone is in Christ, the new creation has come: The old has gone, the new is here! All this is from God, who reconciled us to himself through Christ and gave us the ministry of*

reconciliation:" 2 Corinthians 5:16-18 NIV

All things can't become new if we never put down the old. Not just old life, but old thoughts; old ways of perceiving and experiencing the world. This inactivity of newness, higher consciousness, and greater being is causing fluid and energy blockages within our beings which leads to diseases and disorders. The inactive self is a residence for depression and toxins. When we cannot or have not committed ourselves to assist the body through a liberated expression of who we were created to be, we stop the ability to maintain and restore a healthy flow of life. Eden cannot manifest outside of us, when the desert lives on the inside of us.

We must understand that physical illness, or dis-ease, is first present on an energetic level as a direct result of our beliefs, memories and emotional state.

> *"Since this is the kind of life we have chosen, the life of the Spirit, let us make sure that we do not just hold it as an idea in our heads or a sentiment in our hearts, but work out its implications in every detail of our lives. That means we will not compare ourselves with each other as if one of us were better and another worse. We have far more interesting things to do with our lives. Each of us is an original."* Galatians 5:25-26 MSG

If your mind is a tool, and it is, and you permit your limitless, boundless and measureless spirit to guide it, your physical body will produce fruit that many will not understand. You would have given your body permission to experience what the Spirit gets to experience daily. You then become the window through which the blessings are poured and there won't be room enough to receive. Within you my brother and sister, is a gold mine. These external systems have you on a wild goose chase searching for something outside of you, when they knew it was in you all along. You are the Holy Grail!

Chapter Four

Behind the Veil: The Hidden Secret

Many of you are in uncharted territory, yet in a wide-open field of possibilities. A world unexplored, and an ocean un-sailed. There are changes that will take place in your life because you have collided with destiny. You have built up the courage to move beyond the cross, where everyone around you is standing, and go behind the veil. Going behind the veil is rising above your current surroundings, your existing limitations and problems.

When you go behind the veil, you realize that everything that has become future translates into now. When you project three to five years out in your imagination, you possess the power to come back into the present and begin living it out immediately.

Because we have read the Bible religiously, we have put the body of Christ behind schedule 2000 years. We can see all the miracles of Jesus in the Bible using regular people and now we have the ability to go there in thought and replicate it right now. The little boy with the two fish and five loaves of bread did not know what was about to happen to his lunch, yet he went home with twelve baskets after Jesus fed 5000+ people. We now know because we read what happened, then there is religion, and because of its vices, we can't properly appropriate what took place into current realities. Taking the journey behind the veil now in consciousness, is starting at the twelve baskets and creating your story from there.

Going behind the veil puts you in an advantage because you begin with abundance. You don't have to begin at two fish and five loaves. You and I get to begin at the twelve baskets.

A veil indicates concealment. Like a bride wearing the veil before she makes a covenant and takes on the last name of the groom. The veil is meant to hide her face before the beauty of one connects to another. Until one is ready for knowledge within the kingdom of God, the information that opens the door to unlimited potential, is concealed. Once the veil is your temple *(body)* is rent in twain *(Matthew 27:21)* the application of the knowledge that is now revealed is limited only by your own personal ambitions.

There are no limits on what you can accomplish except for the limits you set for yourself. The more you learn, the more you apply, and then the more you earn. The more you earn, the more you can give. The more knowledgeable you become about the kingdom and its power at work within you, the more courage and confidence you will have to implement what you learn. When you step behind the veil and began to apply what was once concealed, you become virtually unstoppable in everything you do.

Your ideal future can be your present. When you go behind the veil, right now you can capitalize on what would have been your future. Going behind the veil permits you to capitalize on opportunities that would have been provided in your future before anyone can place an obstacle or limitation in your way to try to stop you in your present. Their attempt to stop you in your present will be a failed attempt because you are already in your future. In their reality, you're in your present. In your reality, you're in your future. In God's reality, they are in your past. So, you remain unstoppable!

Kingdom realities remove the veil that prevents you from experiencing your union with divinity. It keeps you from looking outward for something that isn't there when we should be looking inward.

Going behind the veil is designed to reconnect us to our Creator, God. When we make a habit of going behind the veil, we will develop an awareness of our own energetic and powerful self. It revitalizes our bodies and frees us from emotional issues, erroneous belief systems, and physical disorders that no longer serve us.

> *By having the eyes of your heart flooded with light, so that you can know and understand the hope to which He has called you, and how rich is His glorious inheritance in the saints (His set-apart ones)*, Ephesians 1:18 AMP

It is my prayer that through this avenue of revealing truth, you are released from the bondage and deceptions of religion; that you become re-acclimated to living in the abundant environment of Eden. It is my objective to teach you how to take dominion over this world's corrupt systems, instead of serving them as a slave. With these truths, revelations and revolutionary downloads, you will lay hold to God's abundant inheritance and leave behind the past lies of the religious and dogmatic, who remain at the foot of a cross where Jesus isn't any longer.

In the book of Leviticus, we read of the Tent of Meeting. This place of meeting God had three divisions. Each division was represented by certain groups of people. Every court, or gateway was open to only those who were qualified to enter those courts.

There was the Outer Court which is your conscious mind. You use your conscious mind to evaluate new information in comparison to the current knowledge you have, add value to it or devalue it and determine if you will act on it or not. Then there was the Inner Court which is your subconscious mind. Your subconscious mind is the vast bank of data that records every thought, emotion, experience, and every idea that you ever have throughout your life. Whether that of your own or someone else's. Your subconscious mind is not reason; it only obeys your commands.

Lastly, was the Holies of Holies which is your superconscious mind. This is your direct connection to God! All knowledge, and all wisdom dwells here. It can bring you all the ideas and answers you would ever need to achieve anything you set for yourself. This Christ consciousness is the source of all inspiration, intuition, imagination, and yes instinct. The Holy of Holies is in operation in all times and functioning at all times on the inside of you. There is no time where it shuts down.

Going behind the veil, awakens you to this awareness and expands your possibilities that have been lying dormant within you all your life. Life before the veil is superficial; it's a sensory level.

Everything is based on what you can see, hear, taste, smell, and feel. Operating from this level can be unreliable. It produces optical illusions. It's time to take the limits off God which fortunately removes the limitations you have set on yourself!

Say this aloud:

I have no limitations!
There is nothing blocking me.
I get to live in the reality of the Kingdom because God put His heart in my mouth.
I am Heaven's thoughts, words, principles, plans, and patterns of living made visually and verbally manifest on earth.
I am the brightest display of God's glory and the greatest expression of God's personality ever to occur in all eternity in my world.

> *Now unto him that is able to do exceeding abundantly above all that we ask or think, according to the power that worketh in us,* (Ephesians 3:20 KJV)

Everything that has ever been created by humankind in this natural world began in the unseen, imperceptible realm. The very life force that we call God resides in this realm. This realm is what was once hidden behind the veil. The cross of Christ opens us up to this opportunity to experience life behind that veil. It gives us access to what had been hidden from us. However, as a body of believers, we have been stuck at the cross, made a shrine of it, and never went beyond it, which defeats the purpose of Jesus dying in the first place. Remaining at the cross, places His entire message of the kingdom in retirement.

Chapter Five

The Royal Ecosystem Within

With all that you have learned to this moment, you have a choice to make as we move forward. You can choose to be a host to the force of God or a hostage to your ego. Knowing what you want in life is key to your manifesting abilities. You have two choices: one that allows you to create your life by default and the other by design. You manifest by default when you allow the external social environment to tell you what it's best for you to do, be and have in life. When you follow this belief, you abdicate responsibility of most of your choices to an external authority, which you perceive to be more powerful than you are.

If you choose to create by design, you acknowledge that you are the only authority in your life and you are solely responsible of the creation if your life. You do this by shifting your way of looking at reality and manifestation that is not based on competition and achievement, but that is based on understanding that you are already a creative being. You were already created in the image and likeness of God. Do NOT allow anyone to rob you of that!

And God said, Let us make man in our image, after our likeness: and let them have dominion over the fish of the sea, and over the fowl of the air, and over the cattle, and over all the earth, and over creeping thing that creepeth upon the earth.

Genesis 1:26 KJV

God is using me through this medium, to open your mind to higher expectations. By setting higher expectations, you enter into a higher phase of functioning; you think differently. Here is the magnificent thing about the mechanism God gave you, called a brain. It can only do what it thinks it can do. Think about that last statement for a minute. Do NOT just read over that.

YOUR BRAIN CAN DO ONLY WHAT IT THINKS IT CAN DO.

When you understand the law of the mind, you understand that you operate from the seat of your reflective consciousness. This means that your mind is always eavesdropping on your thoughts. As the brain listen to your thoughts, it learns. If you teach your mind limitations, it will become limited. If you teach your mind to see increase and no boundaries, that is exactly what it will begin to manifest.

You must reinforce thoughts of grace, peace, and abundance upon your mind. You must make a choice to take on Jesus' yoke. When you do this, you impose peace upon your mind. You impose, grace and favor upon your mind. You impose a passionate, productive life upon your mind. You put your mind in bondage to God's best! Your mind is submitted to the good life. Your mind is under the authority of total life prosperity. These thoughts must be commanded to have several seats in the room of your reflective consciousness. You have to choose to place your defeated mind on punishment daily.

Let this mind be in you, which was also in Christ Jesus:
Who, being in the form of God, thought it not robbery to be equal with God: Philippians 2:5-6 KJV

When you take on the mind of Christ, you learn to think about the things others are ignoring. When you take on the mind of Christ, you pay attention to what's not obvious. When other people are saying that's crazy, you RUN directly to that. That's an obstreperous mind. That's obstreperous cogitation. That's disruptive thinking or thinking that will get you into trouble with normal people, but it's also the type of thinking that gives you the upper hand in every situation. Glory to God!

I declare that you are released to think creatively!
I declare you are released to think ingeniously!
I decree that you are free to release your resourceful mind, your innovative mind, your artistic mind.
I speak that the Holy Ghost is stimulating your mind for holistic opportunity to bring peace and wealth beyond your own measurement.
With the power of the Holy Ghost, I push forward into unknown territory.

You have to see every day as a new world. This type thinking is obstreperous. It's disruptive. It goes against the rules in place that are only in place to impose pain. It's time for you to think the unthinkable. It's time for you to risk being wrong now in order to be right later. It's time for you to think like others around you aren't thinking. It's time that you do what others around you aren't doing. Which will yield the results that others aren't experiencing.

Even the mystery which hath been hid from ages and from generations, but now is made manifest to his saints: Colossians 1:26 KJV

This mystery has been kept in the dark for a long time, but now it's out in the open. God wanted everyone, not just Jews, to know this rich and glorious secret inside and out, regardless of their background, regardless of their religious standing. The mystery in a nutshell is just this: ***Christ is in you****, so therefore you can look forward to sharing* *in God's glory. It's that simple. That is the substance of our Message. We preach Christ, warning people not to add to the Message. We teach in a spirit of profound common sense so that we can bring each person to maturity. To be mature is to be basic. Christ! No more, no less. That's what I'm working so hard at day after day, year after year, doing my best with the energy God so generously gives me.* Colossians 1:26-29 MSG

Those three words, "CHRIST IN YOU" are so powerful. Christ is NOT Jesus' last name. They didn't have surnames at the time. It was His occupation. Baptist was not John's last name. He had an occupation as a baptizer. That word Christ in its original Greek terminology means, *the anointed one and His anointing*. To anoint means to smear or rub on. The purpose of the anointing once smeared or rubbed on is to remove burdens and destroy yokes. *And it shall come to pass in that day, that his burden shall be taken away from off thy shoulder and his yoke from off thy neck, and the yoke shall be destroyed* ***because of the anointing***. Isaiah 10:27 KJV

As we can see, the purpose of the anointing is to remove burdens and destroy yokes. The term Christ now begins to take shape. This now takes us beyond the famous picture Michelangelo's cousin Ceaser Begoria, a European Catholic, that we were told was Jesus, into the limitless place with God Himself. It drops us into the mind of one who removes burdens and destroys yokes. This is EXTREMELY POWERFUL!

It's time to turn on the switch of your creative consciousness. That super-consciousness that is always at work within you. It's called, the kingdom of God. It is a completely different system that supersedes in system created by man in this world.

Chapter Six

Choose to be Christ-Like

Okay…here we are at what I believe to be the final chapter of this writing. I believe Holy Spirit releases revelation into the lives of people when they're ready to cross the threshold into more consciousness, healing, and awakening. As Albert Einstein says, "problems cannot be solved at the same level of awareness that created them."

"Blessed is the man that walketh not in the counsel of the ungodly, nor standeth in the way of sinners, nor sitteth in the seat of the scornful. But his delight is in the law of the Lord; and in his law doth he meditate day and night. And he shall be like a tree planted by the rivers of water, that bringeth forth his fruit in his season; his leaf also shall not wither; and whatsoever he doeth shall prosper."
Psalms 1:1-3 KJV

In order to get to the ***"whatsoever he doeth shall prosper"*** part of the scripture, we can't just roll by the attributes of being a tree and bearing fruit. This is God taking us, those of us who desire to take part in the ***"whatsoever he doeth shall prosper"*** part of the scripture, into another reality. A completely different system that what the rest of the world is operating from. Being in a position to bear fruit, which is another way of saying, get the results we're desiring, there is an internal process that has to take place. The fruit bearing process of a tree is not external; it's internal before you ever see anything externally.

The most important part of the tree is not visible, it's the root. The root system of a tree spreads out at approximately 2 to 3 times the width of the canopy of the branches. As the roots grow, they look for nutrients and water in the soil, and reach out farther to find them. The farther and deeper the roots travel, the stronger they become, and the more steady and secure they can keep the tree. The root anchors a tree in the soil, keeping it stable and strong so that the harsh winds cannot knock the tree over. Without roots, a tree would wobble, and grow crooked. When roots aren't healthy, it's possible for a large tree to topple over easily even with very little wind or rain. You and I are trees and as a result of empty philosophies od deceased loved one, erroneous teaching of those who meant to keep us ignorant, and some of us just plain ole fear, we have to return to check out root system. To ensure that the fruit we're preparing to yield are so heavy that the tree can't produce them and properly care for them.

My friend, in order to change what is on the surface so you can qualify for the ***"whatsoever he doeth shall prosper"*** part of the scripture , you're going to have to find the source or root, and change things from there. You're going to have to go within, beneath the surface to the root, and everything else will change. Start at the roots, and the leaves won't whither. The only way to make the permanent shifts we desire to make on the outside of our lives is to make them on the inside. It's not arranging things on the outside of your life that is going to make a permanent impact. It's rearranging things on the inside. When you shift on the inside everything on the outside will shift.

Just as the root is the control panel for the tree, consciousness is the control panel for everything in your life. Shifting things from the place of consciousness is like operating from the control room. You can try to control things one at a time, or you can find the control room that is in charge of everything. The more we connect with and enliven the infinite field of consciousness within, which Jesus identifies as the Kingdom of God, *(Luke 17:21)* the more aligned we become with the qualities of that consciousness: expansion, intelligence, creativity, wisdom, and fullness of that consciousness; which is *the mind of Christ.*

To improve the quality of your life, you must improve the quality of your choices. To improve the quality of your choices, you must improve the quality of your thoughts and emotions that produce those choices. To improve the quality of your thoughts and emotions, you must improve the quality of your consciousness. This level of consciousness is the way of thinking that Jesus had to tap into to walk on water, turn water to wine, feed five thousand with two fish and five loaves, and many other acts of being employed from Heaven. He never referred to these things as miracles; He referred to it as work. These actions were not meant to be exclusive to Him. There weren't supposed to be acts that astonished people, it was simply supposed to be the work of those employed to earth from Heaven. Doing big things was supposed to be normal for the believer.

This *mind of Christ* is necessary in order to truly and authentically be Christ-like beyond the idea of just loving one another and tolerating disagreements so we can live together on the planet. Once we get past love, joy, & peace, we can now enter into this reality of the *mind of Christ* or what we can call super-consciousness. Super-consciousness is that level of awareness that we experience when our mind is in a calm and uplifted state. It is the hidden mechanism at work behind intuition, spiritual and physical healing, and successful problem solving.

Let this mind be in you, which was also in Christ Jesus: Philippians 2:5 KJV

Remember what we discussed about the term Christ and its definition is the last chapter. Remember how we spoke on it being in contract with the anointed one and His anointed. We also, gave the biblical definition and purpose of the anointing as the *yoke removing, burden destroying power of God*. So when we hear *mind of Christ*, what we should hear is mind of the burden removing, yoke destroying power of God. When you and I attached and attune to the *mind of Christ*, our thoughts are supposed to be removing burdens and destroying yokes. The level of creative abundance that rests in the place, heald secret for those who would dare believe, is the end all to every problem any human being may face in this world.

Think of yourselves the way Christ Jesus thought of himself. He had equal status with God but didn't think so much of himself that he had to cling to the advantages of that status no matter what.
Philippians 2:5-8 MSG

This is powerful and simple at the same time. It's being able to eat bar-b-que, sweet potato pie, and whatever else that makes you feel and enjoy this human experience and connected to the life here on this place where you've been sent to work called earth, while simultaneously knowing you have another reality that you can tap into at any given moment. This mindset will cause planetary transformation. However, it has to commence with you. When we share this *mind of Christ*, we open ourselves up to the gateways, portals, and expressions of God that will catapult into level of greatness and significance like you've never dreamed of.

God spoke: "Let us make human beings in our image, make them reflecting our nature So they can be responsible for the fish in the sea, the birds in the air, the cattle, And, yes, Earth itself, and every animal that moves on the face of Earth." God created human beings; he created them godlike, Reflecting God's nature. He created them male and female. God blessed them: "Prosper! Reproduce! Fill Earth! Take charge! Be responsible for fish in the sea and birds in the air, for every living thing that moves on the face of Earth. Genesis 1:26-28 MSG

That is pulse-pounding. We reflect the nature of God in the earth. Let that sit for a minute. Don't just read over that. Let those words jump off the page and resonate within your being. Take that in; feel that for a moment. That statement changes the games for everyone! You now begin to create your own reality. You begin to create your own experiences and design your life with what you choose to believe or not believe.

If you choose to create by design, you acknowledge that you are the only authority in your life and you are solely responsible of the creation if your life. You do this by shifting your way of looking at reality and manifestation that is not based on competition and achievement, but that is based on understanding that you are already a creative being. You are already here in this earth to produce, take charge, fill the earth with goodness and good things, and PROSPER!

Chapter Seven

Entry to Manifestation

Why are you laughing? I know I said chapter six was the final chapter, but God wanted something else. I have learned over the years to submit to the will and flow of God's desire. There is obviously more, He desires to use me for your benefit. So stop laughing, this is serious. You're still laughing. This is going to be the final chapter though. I have to be cognizant of information overload. I don't want to put your brain into overdrive and you don't get to work at manifesting your dreams, goals, and aspirations.

"Even the mystery which hath been hid from ages and from generations, but now is made manifest to his saints:" Colossians 1:26 KJV

The term manifest means readily perceived by the eye or the understanding; evident; obvious; apparent; and plain. To manifest something, it must first exist in one place and then appear in another. Even in travel, your name must be on a manifest. When you fly on an aircraft, your name goes on a list that they refer to as the manifest. It identifies and authorizes you to move from one visible place to another visible place. See just because you are physically where you are at this moment, doesn't mean that because India isn't visible right now, it doesn't exist. If you received a passport however, qualifying you to be placed on a manifest, the place India that wasn't once visible becomes visible.

Likewise with your dreams, goals, and aspirations which are already within you ready to be made manifest. They are already on a manifest list ready to be transported from the unseen realm to the seen realm but they need a passport that only you can give them to travel so that you can experience them in this physical realm. In order to do that and do that on a consistent basis however, you must switch systems. There are four types of government; individual, family, church, and civil. The only governmental system able to authorize the travel of your dreams, goals, and aspiration into this physical reality however, is you;

individual government. No democrat, republican, independent, mother, father, sibling, pastor, bishop, apostle, or anyone else can do anything about it. It’s on you!

You have to allow yourself to connect to the ever-flowing frequencies of the Most High, and give those desires authorization to transport from the unseen to the seen. Before they can be made manifest, they have to go through customs, however. Which is indicative to having to navigate through the thoughts, words, and actions that you have become custom to. You can make affirmations all day long. You can think positive thoughts all day. You can shout, dance, and run around the church for hours. None of that will permit those desires to get past the security of those things that are custom to you.

This all goes back to the internal process that we spoke of in the recent chapters. We have to go inside for this. What you desire to happen in life and knowing God has already prepared the place for you to enjoy it, will never manifest itself beyond your familiarities. You're going to have to check what has become familiar to you, because it could very well be what's hindering you and unconsciously blocking access to the best life you could ever experience here on this earth. As we move beyond the familiar humanistic experiences into the spiritual awareness and/or super-consciousness or *mind of Christ*, it places us into a

God-class. Absolutely, I said it! We're not first-class, second-class, or anything else other than God-class. When this becomes the norm for you, you can begin to permit your imagination to flow and then manifestation begins. When the manifestation process gets underway, your God-likeness flips on.

"I have said, Ye are gods; and all of you are children of the most High. But ye shall die like men, and fall like one of the princes." Psalms 82:6-7 KJV

I know those who are not familiar with these type scriptures and even this level of understanding are fussing right now. Your family is going to call you crazy for even reading this much less believing it. Again, it's all your choice. If you share their opinion, you share their lifestyle. So choose wisely. Internally, many could be thinking, how can we be God-like and we've never created a man? That's not true. Stay with me…this is going to bless your socks off. It did for me when God revealed it to me.

The root word to manifest is *man*. So when we *man*-ifest anything from the eternal to temporal we are making man. We are having the same conversation as God had with man when we speak to our future. When we make affirmations, we are standing over the face of the deep of our future and calling in another form of being. When words leave our mouths, as speaking spirits, we are creating man.

It is the spirit that quickeneth; the flesh profiteth nothing: the words that I speak unto you, they are spirit, and they are life. John 6:63 KJV

See God is a Spirit. Jesus says, the words I speak to you are spirit. If we are Christ-like, then the words we speak are spirit. Remember, that breath you use when you inhale and exhale is not yours. It belongs to God. All you have become familiar with is the sound that is connected to it which we call voice. Having sound or voice, doesn't change the fact that the breathe behind the sound is His. It's what He blew into you when He created you and made you like Him. After you became familiar with your voice or sound, you learned to speak words. Well, if you're anything like Him, ***and YOU are***, those words are *Spirit and Life*. So when you speak, the universe around you doesn't recognize the sound as you *BY NAME*, it recognizes the Spirit of the one speaking. You hear you, but the universe hears God. You're hearing God in your voice. When this sinks in, ***LIFE CHANGES TREMENDOUSLY!***

And the **Word** *was made flesh, and dwelt among us, (and we beheld his glory, the glory as of the only begotten of the Father,) full of grace and truth.* John 1:14 KJV

Jesus the ***CHRIST*** is this *WORD* that became flesh and dwelt among us. If we are ***CHRIST***-like, the words we speak will become flesh and dwell among us. The chair you're sitting in right now, is someone's *word becoming flesh and dwelling* among you. The house you're living right now, is someone's *word becoming flesh and dwelling* among you. The automobile you drive right now, is someone's *word becoming flesh and dwelling* among you. The bed you sleep in at night is someone's *word becoming flesh and dwelling* among you. All of these words that are *becoming flesh and dwelling* among us, cost a pretty penny. When we make purchases for these words that have *become flesh and dwelling* among us, we're paying for that persons lifestyle, their children's college, and building their inheritances for their children's children. It's about time you and I become familiar with doing the same.

Christ has set us free to live a free life. So take your stand! Never again let anyone put a harness of slavery on you. I am emphatic about this. The moment any one of you submits to circumcision or any other rule-keeping system, at that same moment Christ's hard-won gift of freedom is squandered. I repeat my warning: The person who accepts the ways of circumcision trades all the advantages of the free life in Christ for the obligations of the slave life of the law.

I suspect you would never intend this, but this is what happens. When you attempt to live by your own religious plans and projects, you are cut off from Christ, you fall out of grace. Meanwhile we expectantly wait for a satisfying relationship with the Spirit. For in Christ, neither our most conscientious religion nor disregard of religion amounts to anything. What matters is something far more interior: faith expressed in love. Galatians 5:1-6 MSG

Those words you just read, now read completely different than they would have without God opening your eyes through the avenues of this book. Your eyes now aren't just looking at the words on the pages, but they are absorbing the energy of the words; the very spirit and life they bring as you read now. Each word now is a stream of light pulsating into your consciousness and you're getting excited about what's next for you. You feel like you can hear me, especially if you've heard my voice before. You feel like I'm sitting right there talking with you. This book you're holding is a *man, a being,* that was given permission to visit with you. By definition, I gave it permission to enter this realm, put its name on the manifest and it has traveled to you. Now read it again and watch what happens.

Welcome to the BRIGHT SIDE!

ABOUT THE AUTHOR

When you hear terms like creative, expressive, innovative and enterprising; you think of Apostle Steven J. Newton Sr., intimately known as "Apostle Steve." Apostle Steve is the President/CEO at The Kingdom Center Global, a global church planting network founded by he and his wife, Christian. Apostle Steven J. Newton Sr. is a celebrated leader of many around the world. Until now, only a fortunate few have been able to draw from the water that God has placed inside of this "well." As God has placed many leading men and women of God in the earth, there is absolutely no substitute for Apostle Steve.

Apostle Steve teaches with an approach of capability without complexity. His ability to tap into the heavens and withdraw spontaneous, pulse-pounding, incisive revelation from God is provocative. The illustrations and information that Apostle Steve uses to coach over 120,000 people all over the globe to the next level in life seem to be organically grown in the Garden of Eden. To sit at the feet of one of such five-star quality of excellence is a pleasurable feast and quite adventurous.

With over 25 years of ministry experience, Apostle Steve's elegant yet practical gift to compel others to live and experience God's best for their lives are far beyond his age. Being groomed for success by many distinguished and well-respected men and women of God across denominational and religious lines, allows him to be an effective communicator in various facets of life. From marriage and family to government and media, Apostle Steven J. Newton Sr., was endowed with a "can't miss" anointing that if the listener follows through with what is heard, results are inevitable.

Apostle Steven J. Newton Sr. has four children, Jer'miya (ladybug) Steven Jr. (tiger), Jamichael (pig), and Victoria (butterfly) and is happily married to his teammate and most wonderful friend, Pastor Christian Newton (formerly Jones) and he lives in Shreveport, LA.

LET'S STAY CONNECTED

I would absolutely love to hear from you!

I enjoy my time in prayer and would get the greatest joy of praying for you.

Send me your information:

Apostle Steven J. Newton Sr.

P.O. Box 29551

Shreveport, Louisiana 71149

ApostleSteve.org

apostlesjn@tkcg.org

Stop by our headquarters location

The Kingdom Center Shreveport/Bossier

Pastors Jeremy & Ebony Lee

701 Pierre Ave

Shreveport, Louisiana 71103

tkcsb.org

I have many other books, curriculum, and modules of instruction to assist you in your journey of transition into the Kingdom Reality. Don't stop here; keep going!

Kingdom Blessings!

Made in United States
North Haven, CT
04 November 2026

21766919R00054